A Kid's Book on Boatbuilding

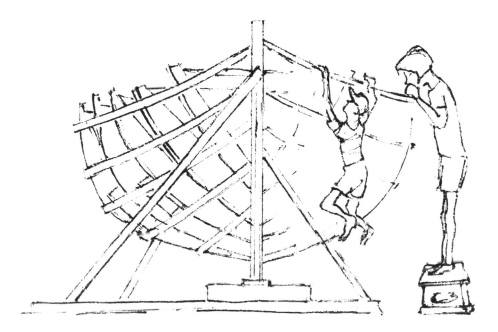

Written and Illustrated by Will Ansel

A WoodenBoat Book

Book design by Lindy Gifford

Printed in Canada

Published by WoodenBoat Publications
Naskeag Road, PO Box 78
Brooklin, Maine 04616 USA
www.woodenboat.com

ISBN: 0-937822-66-3

Library of Congress Cataloguing-in-Publication Data
Ansel, Willits Dyer.
A kid's book on boatbuilding / Will Ansel.
        p. cm.
    ISBN 0-937822-66-3 (pbk. : alk. paper)
    1. Boatbuilding—Juvenile Literature. [1. Boatbuilding.] I. Title.

VM321 .A54 2001
623.8'2—dc21

to D.W.A and E.A.A

Boatshop Cat "Tunafish" snacking

Boats come in many designs, sizes, and shapes.

Some boats are flat-bottomed Like many rowboats

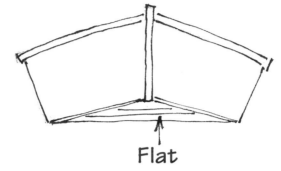

Flat

Some are round-bottomed

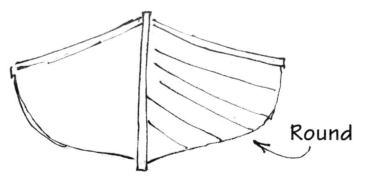

Round

Others are V-bottomed or
Hard-chined

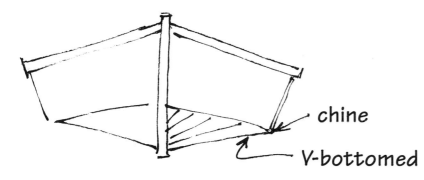

chine

V-bottomed

Some dories are a combination

Round sides,
Flat bottom

What the boat is going to be used
for and what materials you have are
important in deciding what sort of
boat to make.

LOOKING DOWN ON BOATS

Some have a bow & stern

Some don't have sharp bows: Prams, Punts, Scows

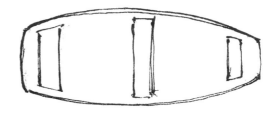

Some are Double Ended: Dories, Canoes, and Whaleboats for example

There are also multi-hulled boats: catamaran

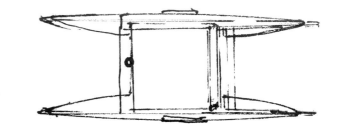

Some boats have decks

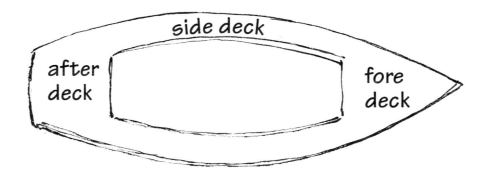

side deck

after deck

fore deck

Small boats such as rowboats, skiffs and dinghies have seats or thwarts to sit on, but no decks…

…and some of the most successful were built in about two days.

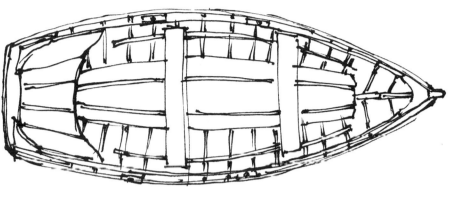

Larger boats may have a shelter with the wheel, controls, and electronics; a cockpit with an engine box; and a cabin, sometimes with bunks, galley, and a head.

Boats may be made of: wood, fiberglass, aluminum, steel, and other materials.

The boat's sides may be lapstrake or carvel (smooth).

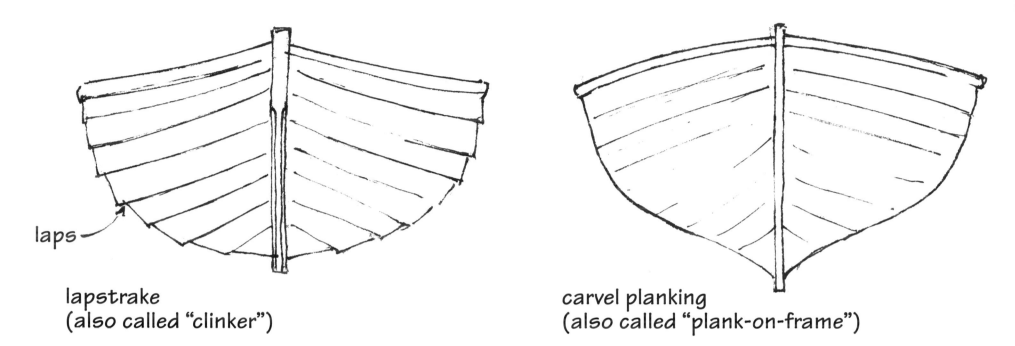

laps

lapstrake
(also called "clinker")

carvel planking
(also called "plank-on-frame")

This book is about round-bottomed, carvel-planked wooden boats.

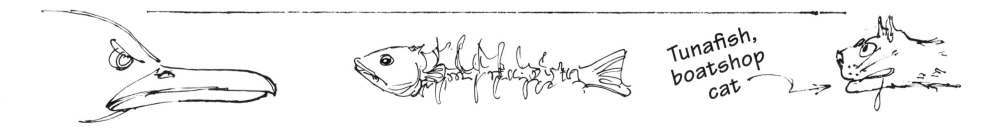

Tunafish, boatshop cat

PLANS

Plans show the shape or lines of a boat, its measurements, and construction. They give all the information a builder needs to make a particular boat.

Plans are drawn on a grid. The measurements along lines of the grid define the shape of the hull.

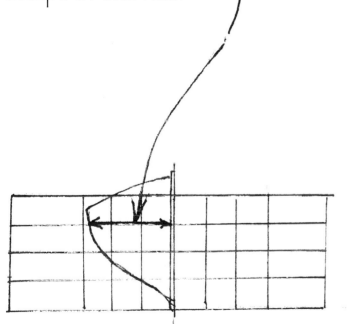

LINES PLANS show the boat's shape.

The **PROFILE** shows it from the side.

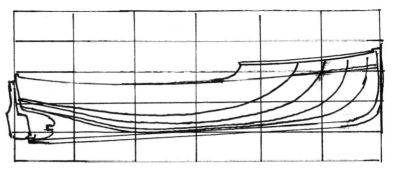

BODY PLAN

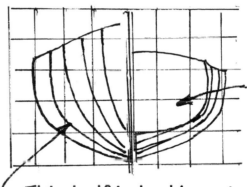

This half shows it from the stern.

This half is looking at the boat from the bow.

PLAN VIEW: looking up from the bottom.

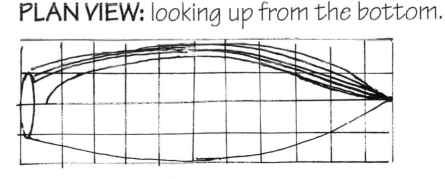

The construction plans show the hull parts and how they go together. There may be other sheets of plans that show sails, spars, rigging, and systems such as electrical wiring.

LOFTING

The builder may loft the lines plan. That means he draws it to full scale—as big as the boat itself. This is usually done on the floor.

From the lofting, he may make patterns and molds. These are temporary, used to make the hull's pieces and parts or to serve as forms to shape and build the hull around.

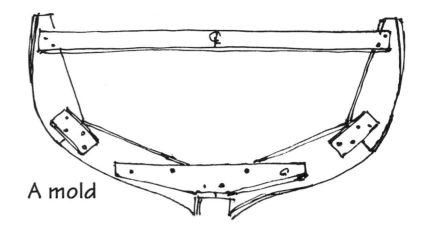

A mold

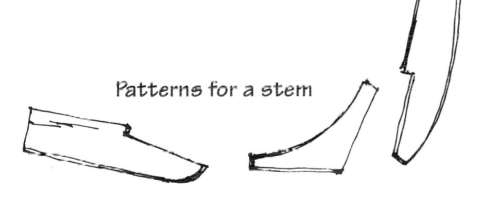

Patterns for a stem

There are other reasons to loft. It checks the plans for "fairness", meaning the hull is not crooked in places. Also, it gives the bevels (for angles) that the edges of some pieces must have to fit. As he lofts, the builder mulls over how it will all go together.

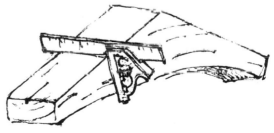

LOFTING (CONT.)

Ducks are lead weights with a bent spike to hold splines (flexible strips, also called battens) to trace along to draw smooth curves.

Boatyards once had moldlofts with a lot of floor space where they lofted huge vessels.

Using the patterns, the keel, stem, knees, and other pieces are marked and cut out. Hand and power tools are used.

Planers and large bandsaws are found in professional shops. They are a great help in shaping the thick oak pieces.

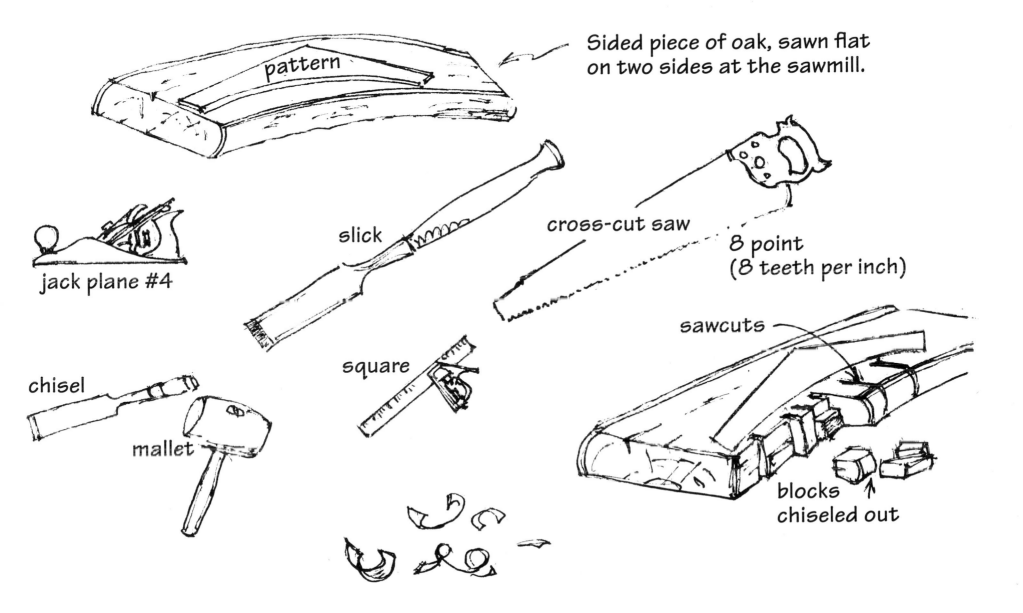

pattern

Sided piece of oak, sawn flat on two sides at the sawmill.

jack plane #4

slick

cross-cut saw

8 point
(8 teeth per inch)

chisel

mallet

square

sawcuts

blocks
chiseled out

The keel is set up on blocks.
The keel is the backbone.

keel

And the stem, stern, deadwood, and
knees are placed and fastened with bolts
and drifts (which are like big rivets).

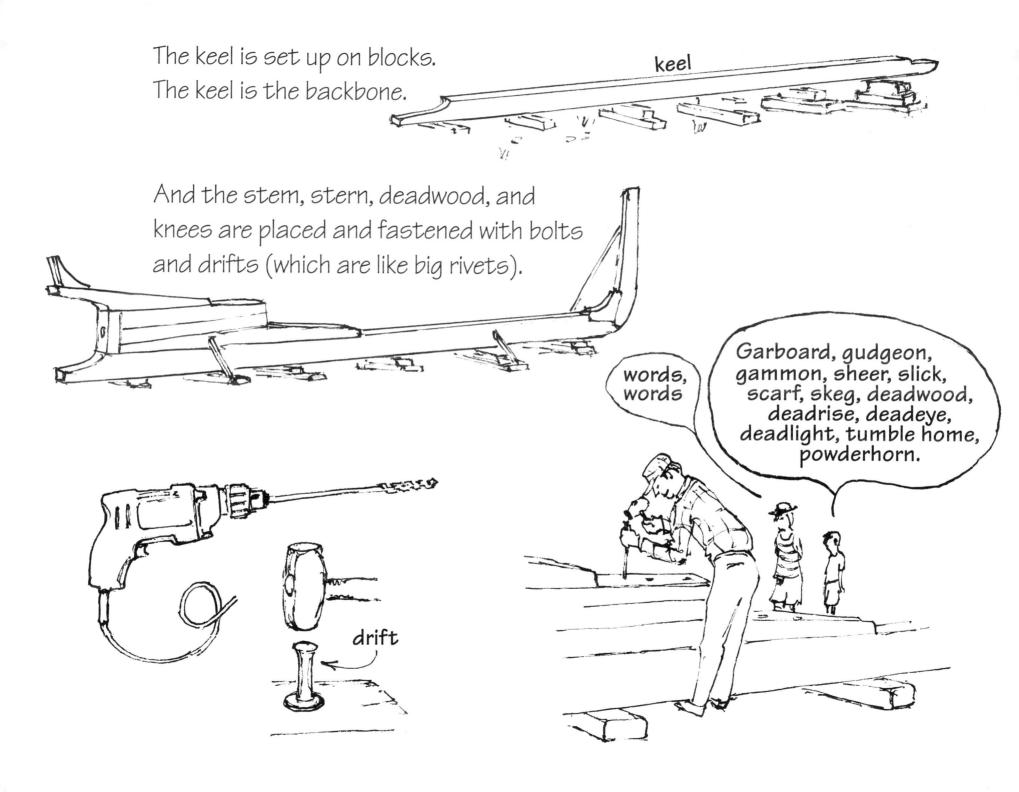

drift

words,
words

Garboard, gudgeon,
gammon, sheer, slick,
scarf, skeg, deadwood,
deadrise, deadeye,
deadlight, tumble home,
powderhorn.

RABBET: Groove running along the keel and up the stem. Edges of the planks fit in it. Getting the right bevel (angle) on the rabbet so the planks fit is not always easy. Builders cut the rabbet with chisels and a rabbet plane.

Dowels are "rods" made of wood. **STOPWATERS** are dowels of pine driven into holes across a seam to keep the water from leaking into the boat through the seam.

DON'T FORGET THE STOPWATERS.

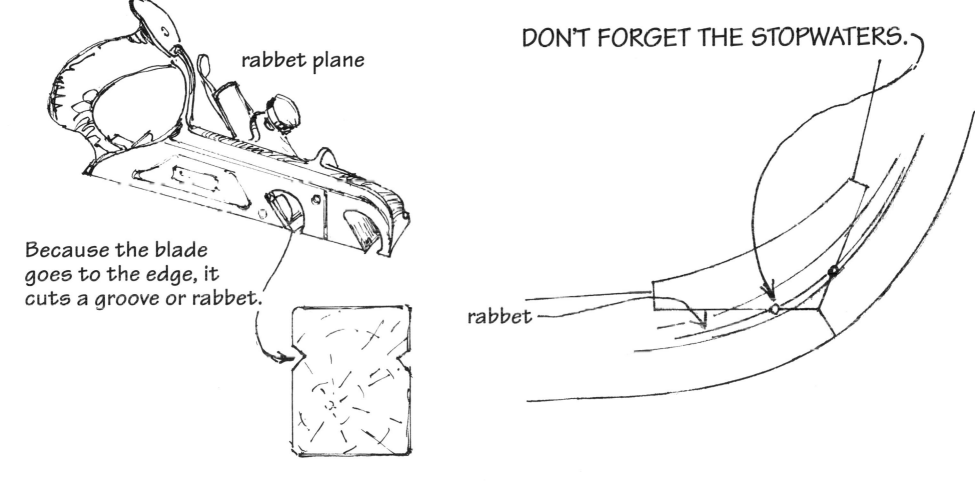

rabbet plane

Because the blade goes to the edge, it cuts a groove or rabbet.

rabbet

The molds are now set up on the keel.
They are not part of the boat itself; they
give form to the hull and later come out.

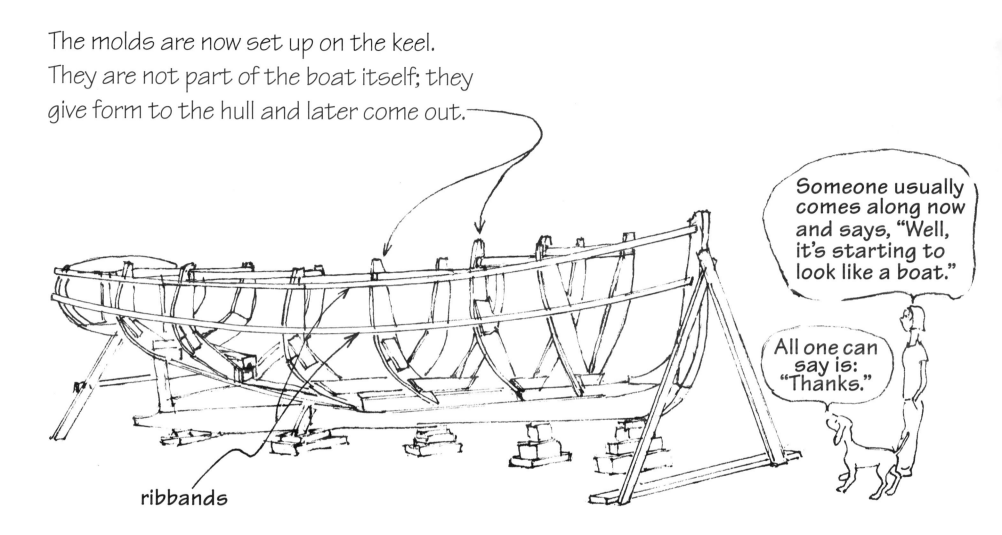

ribbands

Someone usually comes along now and says, "Well, it's starting to look like a boat."

All one can say is: "Thanks."

RIBBANDS are bent around the molds,
eight or ten on each side. They give form,
too, and are temporary. The frames or ribs,
which are a permanent part of the boat,
are steamed and bent inside the ribbands.

STEAMBENDING

If you make a steambox and have a boiler and fire, you can put straight pieces of oak in the box and can steam them and bend them. They stay bent. If the frames are 1 inch thick, you steam about an hour.

When you take the hot pieces out, you have to bend them around something to give them the right curved shape.

Steaming is exciting, even for old boat-builders. It's interesting to see what you can get away with—how many pieces you can do without having one break.

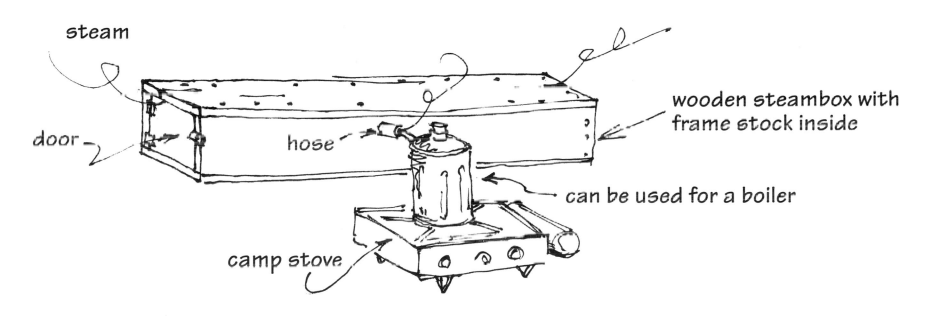

steam

door

hose

camp stove

wooden steambox with frame stock inside

can be used for a boiler

Bending frames usually takes two people—one inside and one outside. They have to work fast while the frames are hot.

hot frame

gloves

They clamp the bent frames to the ribbands.

Puts his foot on it to help bend it.

It doesn't always work. Sometimes frames break.

Never enough clamps, ever.

MORE ON STEAMING

There are some tricks, like beveling the corners of the frames; they break less often if you do. For extreme bends, there is kerfing (making a sawcut up the middle of the piece, thus making two thinner pieces of it), or using a bending strap, a flexible strip of steel clamped on the outside curve of the bend.

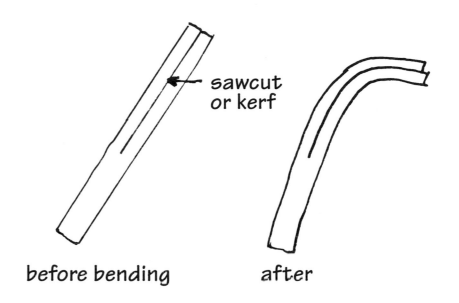

sawcut or kerf

before bending

after

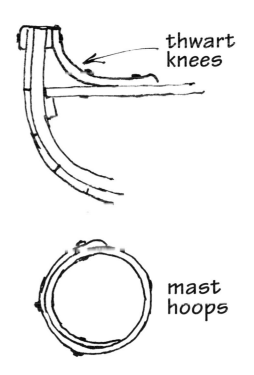

thwart knees

mast hoops

bending strap

oak

Besides frames, you might steam other things. This may be for a stem of a boat, like a canoe or whaleboat.

Masthoops and thwart knees are some other parts made by steambending.

PLANKING

When all the frames are bent and clamped in, the planking can start. The wood for planks is cedar. It is lightweight and slow to rot. Smells good, too.

The planks have to be curved and tapered in a round-bottomed boat, so the edges fit together. If you look at a wooden barrel, you will see that the staves, like planks on a boat, are wider in the middle so the barrel will be round and bulge in the middle; same idea as a boat's planks.

In a boat, the plank near the top, the sheer, usually curve this way, if laid flat:

those in the middle, near the turn of the bilge, are straighter. They are usually narrower:

and those near the keel turn down.

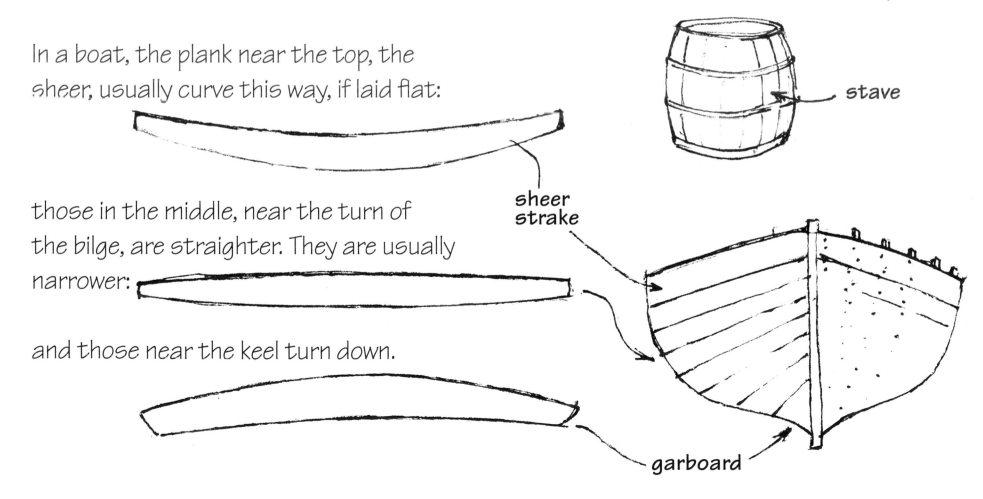

stave

sheer strake

garboard

To get these shapes, boatbuilders **SPILE** a plank pattern, using dividers or a compass.

To spile, you first nail a thin flat board up where the plank you want to shape will fit. It is temporary and is called a spiling batten.

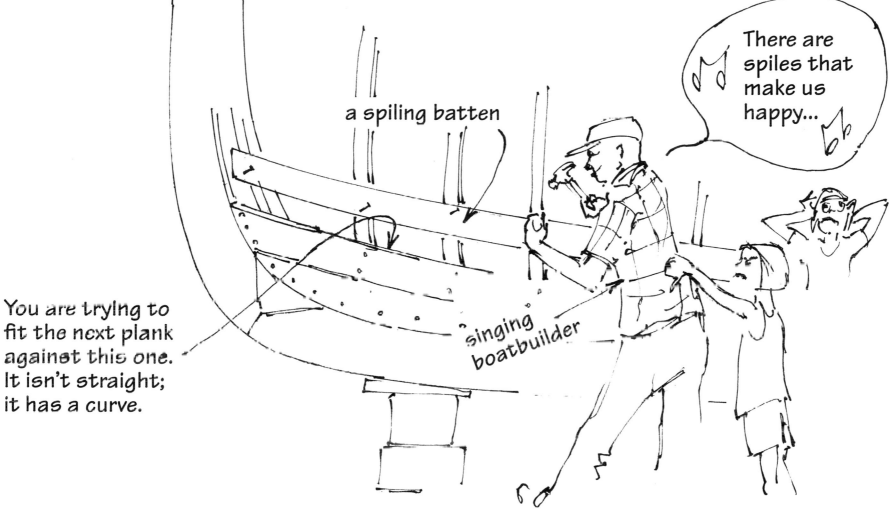

a spiling batten

There are spiles that make us happy...

singing boatbuilder

You are trying to fit the next plank against this one. It isn't straight; it has a curve.

SPILING (CONT.)

Put the point of the dividers on the plank edge and strike a series of arcs.

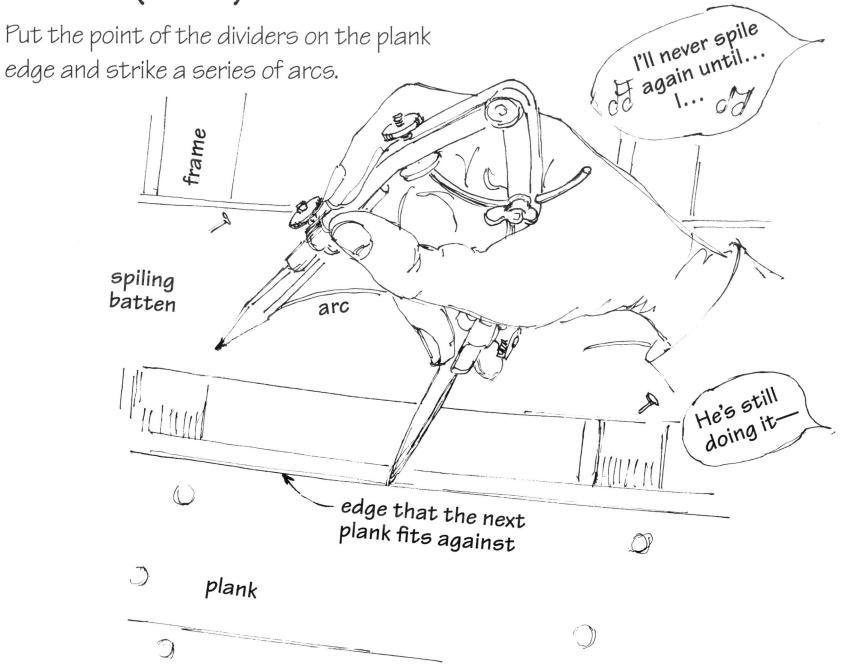

frame

spiling batten

arc

I'll never spile again until... I...

He's still doing it

edge that the next plank fits against

plank

SPILING (CONT.)

Then take the batten off and lay it on the piece of cedar that you are going to use for the next plank.

Turn the dividers around and put the point at two places on each arc...

...and make another set of little arcs that intersect.

...and spring a light batten against them, and then draw a pencil line along it, and you have a curve.

If you saw along that curve, you have the bottom edge, and it should fit the top edge of the plank below.

The whole world spiles with you...

batten

Put light nails in the crosses...

I bet.

There are other ways to spile.

PUTTING PLANKS ON

Some builders start at the keel and work up. Others work towards the middle from top and bottom. The planks are fastened with boatnails, screws, or rivets.

Rivets usually take two people. One person holds a heavy weight against one end of the rivet, and the other person hits the other end with a hammer. Lots of noise, slow, but rivets last a long time.

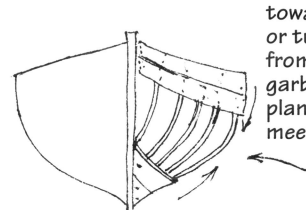

Some builders plank towards the middle, or turn of the bilge, from the sheer and garboard. The last plank, where they meet is the "shutter."

Planks have to be hollowed out to fit against the frames sometimes. This is usually at the turn of the bilge.

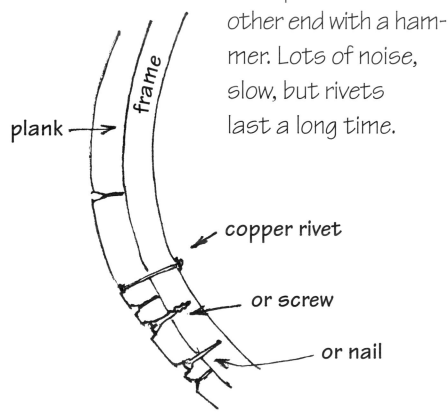

plank →

frame

copper rivet

or screw

or nail

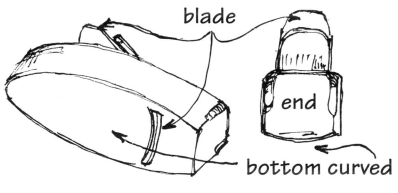

blade

end

bottom curved

wooden backing-out plane can hollow a plank

PLANKING (CONT.)

The planking on both sides goes on at the same time. This way, a plank on one side can be the pattern for its opposite on the other side; also the strains of bending planks are balanced. The boat is more likely to come out symmetrical in shape, not be lopsided.

After the planks are on, the hull is faired, or smoothed, and caulked. **CAULKING** makes the hull tight, keeps it from leaking. Cotton is driven into the seams with caulking irons.

Boatbuilders use some tools other carpenters don't use often, such as backing-out planes to hollow planks, or rabbet planes; dividers and bevel gauges get a lot of use, and all the caulking tools.

NOTE ON BOATSHOP SMELLS

There is a lot to smell around boatshops, like cedar, white pine, yellow pine, white oak, teak, ash, mahogany, oakum, linseed oil, anti-fouling paint, varnishes, solvents, glues, and so on.

Some of these smell good and some don't. Some recall sweaters, cinnamon, tennis shoes, hot southern forests, cigar boxes, low tide, petroleum refineries, etc.

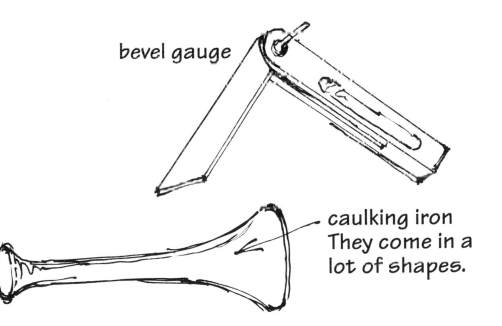

bevel gauge

caulking iron
They come in a lot of shapes.

CAULKING (CONT.)

The caulkers say they can make a bad planking job look good, or at least better. By caulking the tight seams first, the planks are wedged sideways, edgeset. It makes the seams look uniform.

All this is supposed to keep the water out. The planks swell when they soak up water; that helps too.

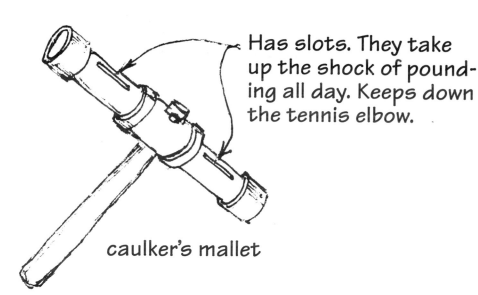

Has slots. They take up the shock of pounding all day. Keeps down the tennis elbow.

caulker's mallet

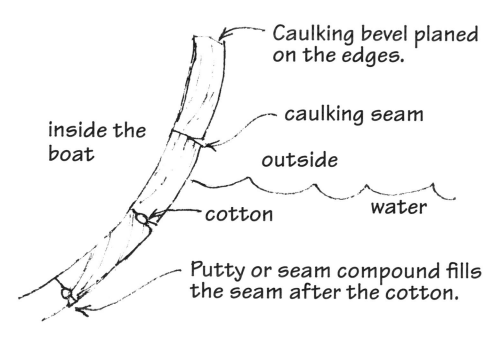

Caulking bevel planed on the edges.

caulking seam

inside the boat

outside

cotton

water

Putty or seam compound fills the seam after the cotton.

Some caulkers put caulking cotton in their ears and a leather ring on their fourth finger that holds and guides the iron, and protects the finger. The noise of caulking is sharp and ringing. By the sound and feel, the caulker knows if the cotton is being set right.

Caulkers make up the skeins of cotton into little bundles they call "kittens."

kitten

SOUNDS IN BOATSHOPS

A boatshop can be a noisy place. Some boatbuilders use ear protection, and more probably should. Besides the usual din of power tools, there are the distinctive sounds of caulking and riveting.

A caulking mallet with a head of live oak or mesquite and steel rings is prized for its sound. A mallet is either good-sounding or not, to the caulker's ear. He pays a lot for a good one.

He's drilling holes and driving copper nails.

He's boring and riveting.

Can he be both?

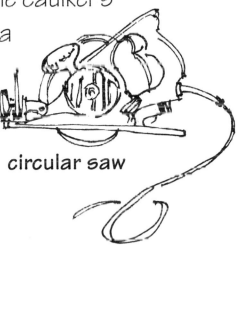

circular saw

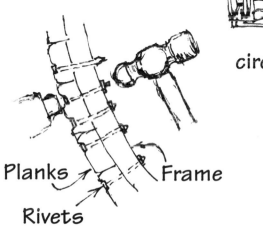

Planks   **Frame**

Rivets

Putting heads on rivets is another noisy operation. It is done by hammering with a ballpeen hammer with light, rapid taps. After a dozen or so taps, the rivet has a head on top of a burr, and the boatbuilder moves on to the next rivet. There are a few hundred to do in even a small boat, but rivets are good fastenings, and a line of neat rivet heads is satisfying.

DECKS

Small, open boats, like rowboats, don't have decks. Larger boats with cabins, deckhouses, hatches, and cockpits do. The decks are supported by deckbeams. These go across (athwart) the boat, and rest on the clamps.

Deckbeams are crowned, or curved. Water runs off and they are stronger because of crown.

Decks add a lot of strength to a boat. It is important that they are tight, so they are caulked and sometimes covered with canvas.

Decks that leak cause rot inside and misery, especially if they leak over your bunk (plywood covered by fiberglass is one solution).

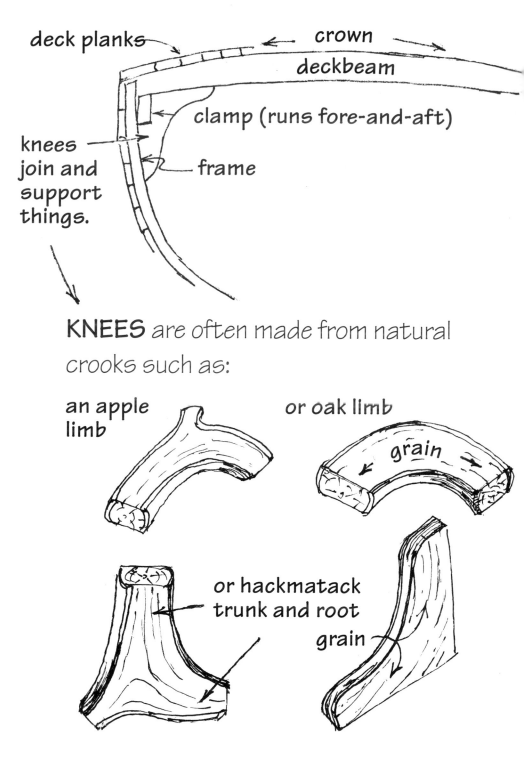

deck planks crown deckbeam
clamp (runs fore-and-aft)
knees join and support things. frame

KNEES are often made from natural crooks such as:

an apple limb   or oak limb   grain

or hackmatack trunk and root   grain

AND OTHER THINGS

After the coamings, deckhouses, rails, and other carpentry work on the hull is done, there is still about ½, or more, of the work to do. There may be mast and rigging, joinery work such as bunks and lockers below, and electrical and other systems. For example, if the boat is to have an engine there must be, beside the engine itself, the engine mounts, a shaft and propeller, bearings, controls, gauges, tanks, fuel lines, exhaust system, pumps, through hull valves, and batteries.

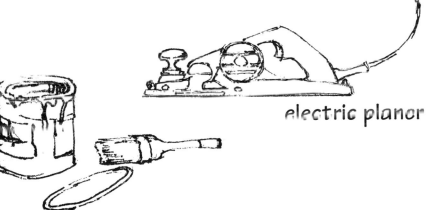

electric planer

Building a boat can get complicated— but at last it is launched. A lot of work often continues after the launching. The launching is a big moment, though.

spoke shave

LAUNCHING

The old way usually had the boat on a cradle that sat on rollers and planks, and the whole works were shoved in with a heave. Nowadays, boats are often launched from a big trailer on a ramp or by a travellift. These methods have less drama, but more control; it things are really going wrong, all can be stopped and reversed.

Probably most boatbuilders would prefer launching in secrecy with no crowds, but they don't get off that easily. A builder doesn't want to be pinned down to a

date, and may have nagging doubts about having forgotten something important.

A lot of launchings are just fine with the bottle breaking at the first swing, flags, the tide and weather right, no speeches, and the boat left floating quietly on her lines.

The bottle doesn't have to be smashed. You can just pour it on.

If you are interested in learning more
about the world of wooden boats, please
visit our website: www.woodenboat.com.

As a kid, Will Ansel would spend hours rowing the creeks around Annapolis, Maryland. From his boat he could look down on the wrecks of Chesapeake skipjacks, and watch the turtles sun themselves on deckbeams and the tops of centerboard trunks. He found other types of Chesapeake boats there too, including the old "log" boats. Years later, Will built scaled-down skipjacks, wrote about them, and eventually went to work at Mystic Seaport as a ships' carpenter and boatbuilder. Will now lives in Georgetown, Maine, in an old house built at the water's edge, with a small shop and dock. The inventory of boats and kayaks is currently seven. Besides keeping up, using, and adding to these, he does some writing and painting, and work around a cabin in the woods.